BLUE?

Glenview, Illinois • Boston, Massachusetts • Chandler, Arizona
Shoreview, Minnesota • Upper Saddle River, New Jersey

See the light?

It is yellow.

Trucks get set to stop.

2

The light is red.

Trucks stop.

They stop on the wet street.

4

Jack will not.

Trucks sit on the wet street!

It is a truck jam!

I will go on blue.

I do not like red, yellow, green!

I like blue best.

Jack heard a big blast.

Is it Rosie?

It is Big Rig!

I will go!

I will go fast!

I like green!